"Ran Walker sees and sews these poems
with a sharp quill. Keen eyes. Talent.
His poems are Black, blues, and all
things in crawl spaces in the middle.
Take time to sit with these gems.
Mine them. Mind them. Hear how they
fire like gun blasts on the page."

—Van G. Garrett, author of *Songs in Blue Negritude* and *49: Wings & Prayers*

"It's no surprise that [Ran Walker's] heroes
are those who are unsung or those who we
only have a surface understanding of. My
childhood hero, given his graffiti-slinging
name, SAMO is memorialized in all his
complexity. A time-traveling Baldwin lingers
in between simile. The hashtags who were
names, stories, and relatives etched into our
hearts float through each page."

—Erica Buddington, HBO Def Poet and
Founder of The Langston League

"The Kwansaba form of sevens (seven lines, seven words per line, no word with more than seven letters) was created by Dr. Eugene Redmond, a poet and cultural critic, specifically to praise African Americans and Black culture. Each of Ran Walker's Kwansabas accomplish this goal. From the first poem honoring his father, 'Randolph Rhymes with Landolph' to the James Baldwin, Toni Morrison, and Richard Wright tributes, to the Sean Puffy Combs (aka P. Diddy) poem that succinctly explores the icon's evolving image from a hip-hop artist to a mogul to a brand, to the Black Lives Matter poems, this book informs as well as delights.

"With a simplistic strength and fighting courage, *Most of My Heroes Don't Appear on No Stamps* celebrates black life. Walker's Kwansabas are both an examination of the past, yet a kind of foundation for where the Black community can go."

—Shonda Buchanan, author of *Equipoise: Poems from Goddess Country* and *Who's Afraid of Black Indians?*

Most of My Heroes Don't
Appear on No Stamps

Most of My Heroes Don't Appear on No Stamps

Kwansabas
by Ran Walker

This book is published by
University of Hell Press
www.universityofhellpress.com

Cover and Interior Design
by Vince Norris
www.norrisportfolio.com

Published in the
United States of America
ISBN 978-1-938753-33-6

Author's Note

During the summer of 2006 I was looking forward to completing my transition from small town attorney to college professor. It was during that time that I participated in the Hurston/ Wright Writers Week in Washington, DC. While there I became friends with a poet named Van G. Garrett. It was Van who first told me what a Kwansaba was, but seeing myself as primarily a fiction writer, I would take another six years before I began to write Kwansabas of my own.

When Dr. Eugene Redmond created the Kwansaba in 1995, it was designed to ultimately serve as a praise poem for African-American culture. The non-rhyming form was styled to contain seven lines, seven words per line, and no word of more than seven letters (with foreign words and proper nouns getting an exemption here). Up until I wrote my first Kwansaba, the only poetic forms

I had explored were Italian sonnets, haikus, and free verse. Still, there was something alluring about this form.

Forty-nine words. What could I say in so few words? Well, apparently a lot. I wrote quite a few of them and ultimately decided to use a number of them in my novel *Daykeeper*. It was only when I met Eve Connell and talked with her about my work that it even crossed my mind that I had written a book's worth of them.

The collection you now hold in your hands covers many topics, ranging from interrogations of celebrity culture to issues that speak directly to the Black Lives Matter movement. There are seven sections of seven poems each.

It is my hope that you enjoy these poems and that they will resonate with you in at least some small way.

Peace,
Ran

For Elle and Zoë

TABLE OF CONTENTS

NATIVE SONS

Randolph Rhymes with Landolph

Born in Oak Grove, the last of
eight to Henry and Annie, a twin
who'd one day head to college, then
on to law school, marry my mother,
then have my brother and me. He
said his name didn't come from Hearst;
it just rhymed with his twin sister's.

Richard Wright Bids Farewell

So long, Natchez, ghost of my youth;
Paris lures me with her open arms,
telling me my words are not foreign,
unlike at home, where even reading is
a sin and my words are hidden
like Easter eggs in freshly mown grass,
waiting for future readers to find them.

Gordon Parks Photographs the World

He saw through the lens of time,
bending light at its various angles, holding
faces on film, smoke dancing white from
pipe beneath heavy silver whisker, aged hands
shaping music from jagged shards of opal
so that we might see the beauty
of all that is waiting within us.

Remembering Basquiat

SAMO carried cans of spray paint, making
art of noise—ready to attack any
wall in sight, the nappy crown-covered
demons of his mind dancing like a
crayon-toting child on acid. SAMO, black
Bo-Ho, clad in Armani and wooden clogs,
riding atop the muted gallops of Horse.

The Fire This Time

We did not know Baldwin had a
crystal ball and could tell our crooked
future with typed words, while smoking a
fag in some French house, his finger
still on our fragile pulse, telling us
this pain is nothing new, that our
Black will always be blue like Sonny.

The Audacity of America

Toni told us the man from Hope
was Black, back when we only sought
to be seen and have our hue
valued; now we have a man of
hope, who sees what *We* can be,
using the wings of Solomon to soar,
and show us what *change* really means.

Rumble, Young Man, Rumble

I was born to rumble in rings
across the world, my heart a fist,
guided by Allah, to destroy those who
would be bigger or would hit harder.
No longer Cassius, who betrays his brother,
I elevate as Ali, greater within myself,
forever ready to take on all comers.

WINDOW SEAT

Donuts

Cold, musty scents of old books, ghosts
roaming ivory towers, as we invoke séances
from closed canons, reading closely those pages
that revive the souls of our heroes
and glaze the eyes of each student
like sweet orbs of Krispy Kreme donuts
falling into neatly amassed rows and boxed.

Envy

I teach through the thick haze of
clouded night, the pupils of my pupils
fixed on their cell phones as they
yearn to connect to others like silk
strands of web dancing from a spider's
abdomen, casting glowing nets across the sky
between broad tree limbs I so envy.

On Days When I Remember I Am a Lawyer

Some days I marvel that they allow
me to stand in front of kids
and help them shape how they see
the world. In another life, I would
stand before some judge, arguing some case,
and wish I were in a room
ready to teach writing to bright minds.

Summer Journaling

The heat of summer rolls upon me,
dotting my face with pearls of sweat,
cooking my thirsty mind ever so slowly,
while my parched ideas haunt this pen.
My ink is blue like indigo oceans
kissing ivory shores where birds soar freely,
dancing upon the white of this page.

(Bluest Horizon)

Bluest horizon, ocean meeting sky as summer
fades into fall, breeze crisp like an
ironed shirt. This is now our home,
where our dreams will flow like tides
licking the sands of the August beach.
I stand here this morning, pen in
hand, ideas dancing across an azure morning.

365 ¼ Days

Each year I get older, they get
younger. I used to be fresh, too,
eyes wide open, looking to learn things
I didn't already know, to be young,
gifted, and Black, like Donnie before the
ledge or raisins drying in the sun,
but I, too, must gray and evolve.

Pen-ultimate

Between my hand and the page, this
pen, the next to last refuge of
the idea, before it becomes complete, final
like an exam for a course you
forgot you were even taking, dreams chasing
you toward your art, away from those
who don't care to know your truth.

BLACK   MATTER

Page Six

I try not to get angry when
people make light of a Black life
snuffed out so plainly. He must have
done wrong/he should have/what did
he expect (being unarmed and Black and
not knowing his place)? His face, his
race, buried in *The Daily*, page six.

He Mattered

I'd never seen a body my age,
eyes and lips glued shut, a silence
loud as mothers' muffled screams against still
chests; no more sighs or laughs or
nods goodbye, just a shell of my
memory, a photo on a faded program,
another hashtag they'll forget about next week.

Advice from Father to Son

Keep your hands at ten and two.
That way they can't say you reached
for a pocket knife or water gun,
any weapon of their minds, because Black
men's hands look like more than hands
to those who would shoot first when
fingers ball into a fist to resist.

Legions

I beat my fists against a sky
filled with legions of our black angels,
praying you see a man, not a
monster, whose talons scrape at your idea
of the American dream. You move, gun
drawn, ready to fire your hate into
my soul—but I refuse to die.

What Kap Ponders on the Sideline

Why do they hate me so much?
Is it because I choose to fly
my colors at half-mast, a banner,
crimson like blood, sevens on each side?
Or does my afro scare them, rising
up, round like a Black Power fist,
asking that my sons not be ignored?

A Simple Question from a Concerned Father

Hold on. Let me get this right:
I can't drive while I am Black.
I can't sit while I am Black.
I can't kneel while I am Black.
I can't live while I am Black.
Well, what should I tell my little
girl about the value of her skin?

The Jilting of Darfur

Her dress, a petal snagged on thorns,
ripped dreams aflame like burnt black doves.
Thrown rice feels like small razor blades,
as blood-soaked cotton covers her thighs.
"Love me!" is her long, wailing cry,
but he sneers his broad diamond grin,
machete raised high for babies to see.

OF BEATS AND MELODIES

Coltrane's Tenor Sax

Fingers that could tickle a lover's side
caress the eager keys of hollow brass,
calling forth a sweet, simple melody, a
chant: *a love supreme—a love supreme—*
running his fire on tracks of ice,
molding wind into sound and sound into
modal dreams kissed by Miles and Bird.

**Only the Godfather of Soul Can Jump Back
and Kiss Himself**

It was always the feet that caught
the rhythm and twisted it through his
body, feet that once walked dusty Georgia
roads and slid across the Apollo stage
and arenas in Zaire. Lived in America,
atop horns, drums, bass, and wicked guitars,
and left prints in our soulful dreams.

The 21st Night of September

Badeya, the deep groove of Kemetic funk—
wishing I could be so fly on
a pyramid wall, my name a note
hummed by Maurice White over a kalimba.
Soaring like the golden wings of Heru,
song of the son of the Sun,
I dance and rejoice in this Fantasy.

The Black Stars of Bed Stuy

Dante and the True Student plugged in,
flowing in Native Tongues, against murals of
fallen MCs, lifting mics like fat blunts
to elevate lost souls. They be Raw—
Kus truth will not be touched up
like pics of video vixens, yet some
Bush Niggas still live ready to die.

The Lost Boys of South Bronx

Remixed voices, coarse as jagged cinder blocks,
yet quick as blown razor blades, blood
on young tongues (they spit red poetry),
not calling for change, just dollar bills.
Their heroes don't appear on no stamp,
and Reagan's over a million miles away,
so why *not* let this mutha burn?

Esperanza Walks Her Bass

She holds the sturdy curves upright, fingers
walking tones down a fret, like fairies
dancing along the petals of morning lilies,
her afro, like the sun's crown, glowing,
her voice as light as an eyelash
kissing a soft, bare cheek, this voice
merging treble and bass into one clef.

Down at the Crossroads

Wind-blown cotton strewn along Highway 61
like tissue banners torn by frat boys,
the sun presses me down to earth
like a huge forearm against my neck.
Fingers pluck strings to shake the ghosts
from trees. They say Papa Legba lives
around here—but I've never seen him.

ALL THE WORLD'S A STAGE

Diddy, Inc.

No more neon shiny suits, just labels
on records, on clothes, on cologne bottles,
on any product that can be sold—
no longer a man, only a brand,
a symbol of a bold new culture,
one born of hip hop, open-sourced
and remixed to play on your iPhone.

Public Enemy No. 1

Chuck D's voice, full of fire and
fury, Flavor Flav, the jester, dancing in
time to Terminator X on the Wheels
of Steel, and Brooklyn pulsing like bass
beneath the shaky bricks of a place
on fire, Spike's camera on a crane,
double dolly shot, then cut to pan.

Bey Hive

The hive swarms when she wakes up,
thirsty for the latest glimpse into her
world, buzzing at pics and posts of
glamour framed in a box marked private.
They watch the queen drizzle her honey
across the stage, leaving sticky traces of
Texas nectar running down their waiting petals.

Buggin' Out Tries to Keep His Dick Hard in a Cruel and Harsh World

Please, baby baby, please, don't step on
these Jordans, 'cause they are part of
my ID, like Sal's slices, leg weights,
these specs, this swagger, and my hair.
Scuffin' these 4s is like taintin' my
soul, and that's all a brother has
when the Wall of Fame burns down.

The Dilemma of Luke Cage

They don't know what to do with
you, big Black man, hero-for-hire.
They pimp your dreams for three dollars
and steer your world through blue eyes,
but at least they made you strong,
like your people, skin like steel, but
if Kal-El can fly, why can't you?

Princess Shuri

What would Wakanda be without her touch,
making miracle after miracle with science, her
lips dancing into a broad, knowing smile?
She wears her royalty in the braids
that cascade down her slender ebony back,
ready to protect her brother, her country,
with the power of her many gifts.

Toni Pens the Song of Milkman

I want to fly on my own
wings, soaring against the sour taste of
mother's milk and the loss of faith
that cloaks me like a death shroud,
burying me blindly in my family's name
so that I fight my only friend
to avoid the fate of my father.

GUILTY FEET HAVE GOT NO RHYTHM
OR
TREV AND KAT'S BRIEF BROOKLYN
LOVE AFFAIR

A Day in the City

They stood near the bridge, daring the
other to make the first move, lean,
lips pushing into nervous space, hoping to
touch the other's, and feel the tender,
soft warmth of desire, the blanket against
a cool autumn dusk, marking the genesis
of the magic they hoped to create.

The Conjurer

I wish there were words to erect
a place where ideas could come alive
and mingle with desires, like flavors of
you and me, this caramel sundae of
we, sweet like Sunday morning nectar. We
move letters into sounds, breath, and whisper,
shaping ecstasy into life on this page.

Passion

Soft whisper, wet with lust, we taste
each other, tongue against tongue, fingers dancing
across necks, making bread crumb trails for
each kiss to follow. We swallow each
other, breath by breath, and watch bodies
tingle from orgasm, memory strong with the
passion of two souls uniting against fate.

Insomnia

To let her go is to admit
she was once mine, which she wasn't—
maybe in dreams where her arms reached
for me to comfort her and help
fill the space broken hearts often leave.
Now she is gone, making a void
in her wake, and I cannot sleep.

Icebox

Cool winter air whips across my face
making me long for warm hands to
caress my body and shield away this
frigid space. I relive sunrays dancing in
her eyes on an auburn evening, her
smile gentle as the first sweet kiss
that still lingers long after she left.

Goodbye

She took a piece of me with
her, my words packed tightly beneath clothes
and worn photos and books yet read.
I wonder if my lips will be
the last memory to fill her bag
as she packs away her past and
tastes the freedom she has longed for.

Il était une fois

Once upon a time, I knelt between
your thighs, hungry for the taste of
rain, wet like tears from missing you,
the soft whisper of your petals calling,
like a siren to sink what was
left of the ship that carried my
soul, holding what was left of us.

FOR LAUREN

Diggin'

Her voice drips through the seams in
my mind; I am wanting to make
her mine, like feelings of a first
kiss beneath broad tree limbs that cast
shadows over young nervous faces. She is
a melody taking form, her tune dancing
in my mouth like an ancient chant.

Saturn

The glow of the sun behind your
hair, curly brown, a smile, a wink—
I revolve, slowly at first, just another
planet, but now I rotate to your
melody, cosmic groove of love so wide
it wraps me like Saturn's rainbow rings,
no dust and ice, just your arms.

Elemental

I marvel that I can lose myself
in a single kiss, unable to find
the shore beyond this liquid abyss. You
are the sky, steady beyond my eyes,
safety from the cynical storms that rumble
across the plains of my past, the
answer to the query I never asked.

You Are the Perfect Verse over a Tight Beat

Love is a track that gets remixed
each day, modeled to the lyrics spat
from our hearts, the melody holding fast
against the kind of change we cannot
avoid. We evolve the way grooves often
do, the bass and snare locked into
endless dope breaks over which we flow.

Remembering How She Knocked Me off My Feet

I see us in the park, lying
beneath the canopy of an old tree.
Her head on my chest, she savors
Zora or Alice or Toni or Gloria.
I touch her hand and she smiles,
letting me know that we're still classic
like *Songs in the Key of Life*.

Standing at the Altar

I stand, heart racing, looking for words
to lift from my knotted stomach, lips
parted like blinds longing to pull light
through windows of my anxious soul, not
knowing why I am nervous, because I
realize I can now imagine forever, even
as the pastor signals us to kiss.

Zoë

Like Stevie said, she was made from
love, along with the best that you
and I have to offer this world,
our own miracle, the answer to prayers
sprung beyond clasped fingers and open lips,
a song made for dancing in spring,
when life is anew with our dreams.

ACKNOWLEDGMENTS

The following poems have been previously published: "Legions" (*Black Lives Have Always Mattered*, 2 Leaf Press), "Remembering Basquiat" (*Phati'tude Literary Magazine*), "The Lost Boys of South Bronx" (*Phati'tude Literary Magazine*), "Richard Wright Bids Farewell" (originally published as "The Ghosts of Natchez: For Richard Wright" by *DrumVoices Review*), and "Only the Godfather of Soul Can Jump Back and Kiss Himself" (originally published as "Those Feet" in *Say It Loud: Poems About James Brown*).

I would like to extend thanks to my parents, my brother, my in-laws, my co-workers, and my fellow creatives for all their continued support and encouragement.
Special thanks to Eve Connell for seeing something in my poems worth sharing with the world and to Greg Gerding for including me in the University of Hell

Press family.

Last, but by no means least, I would
like to thank my wife for loving and
putting up with me, and my daughter,
who inspires me to continue writing no
matter what.

AUTHOR BIO

Ran Walker is the author of sixteen
books. His short stories and poetry have
appeared in a variety of anthologies.
Prior to becoming a writer and educator,
he worked in magazine publishing and
practiced law in Mississippi.

Ran is a graduate of Morehouse College
(BA in English), Pace University (MS
in Publishing), and George Washington
University Law School (JD), and is the
recipient of both a 2005 Mississippi
Arts Commission/NEA artist grant
and a 2006 artist mini-grant. He has
also served as an Artist-in-Residence
with the Commission. In addition, he
is a past participant in the Hurston-
Wright Writers Week Workshop and is
the recipient of a fellowship from the
Callaloo Writers Workshop.

Ran is an Assistant Professor of English
and Creative Writing at Hampton
University, and lives in Virginia with his
wife and much better half, Lauren, and
his amazing little rockstar daughter, Zoë.

THIS BOOK IS ONE OF THE
MANY AVAILABLE FROM
UNIVERSITY OF HELL PRESS.
DO YOU HAVE THEM ALL?

by **Jason Arment**
Musalaheen

by **Tyler Atwood**
*an electric sheep jumps to greener
pasture*

by **John W Barrios**
Here Comes the New Joy

by **Eirean Bradley**
*the I in team
the little BIG book of go kill yourself*

by **Suzanne Burns**
Boys

by **Calvero**
someday i'm going to marry Katy Perry
i want love so great it makes Nicholas
Sparks cream in his pants

by **Nikia Chaney**
us mouth

by **Leah Noble Davidson**
Poetic Scientifica
DOOR

by **Rory Douglas**
The Most Fun You'll Have at a Cage
Fight

by **Brian S. Ellis**
American Dust Revisited
Often Go Awry

by **Greg Gerding**
The Burning Album of Lame
Venue Voyeurisms: Bars of San Diego
Loser Makes Good: Selected Poems 1994
Piss Artist: Selected Poems 1995-1999
The Idiot Parade: Selected Poems 2000-2005

by **Lauren Gilmore**
Outdancing the Universe

by **Rob Gray**
The Immaculate Collection/The Rhododendron and Camellia Year Book (1966)

by **Joseph Edwin Haeger**
Learn to Swim

by **Lindsey Kugler**
HERE.

by **Wryly T. McCutchen**
My Ugly & Other Love Snarls

by **Michael McLaughlin**
Countless Cinemas

by **Johnny No Bueno**
We Were Warriors

by **Isobel O'Hare**
all this can be yours
(hardcover & paperback)

by **A.M. O'Malley**
Expecting Something Else

by **Stephen M. Park**
High & Dry
The Grass Is Greener

by **Christine Rice**
Swarm Theory

by **Liz Scott**
This Never Happened

by **Michael N. Thompson**
A Murder of Crows

by **Ellyn E. Touchette**
The Great Right-Here

by **Sarah Xerta**
Nothing to Do with Me

edited by **Cam Awkward-Rich & Sam Sax**
The Dead Animal Handbook: An Anthology of Contemporary Poetry

CPSIA information can be obtained
at www.ICGtesting.com
Printed in the USA
FFHW012349030319
50780092-56205FF